The Disappearances

Poems

AF673592

Vijay Seshadri

HarperCollins *Publishers* India

First published in hardback in India by
HarperCollins *Publishers* in 2007
First published in paperback in 2014
4th Floor, Tower A, Building No. 10, Phase II,
DLF Cyber City, Gurugram, Haryana -122002
www.harpercollins.co.in

1 2 3 4 5 6 7 8 9 10

Copyright © Vijay Seshadri 2007, 2014

ISBN: 978-93-5136-775-8

Wild Kingdom first published by Graywolf Press 1996
The Long Meadow first published by Graywolf Press 2004

Vijay Seshadri asserts the moral
right to be identified as the author of this work.

All rights reserved. No part of this publication may be reproduced,
stored in a retrieval system, or transmitted, in any form or by any means,
electronic, mechanical, photocopying, recording or otherwise,
without the prior permission of the publishers.

Typeset in 12/16 Cochin
Nikita Overseas Pvt. Ltd.

Printed and bound in India by
Manipal Technologies Limited, Manipal

The Disappearances

Vijay Seshadri was born in Bangalore in 1954 and went to the USA at the age of five. His collections of poems include *3 Sections*, which won the 2014 Pulitzer Prize for Poetry, the James Laughlin Award winner *The Long Meadow*, *Wild Kingdom* and *The Disappearances*. His poems, essays and reviews have appeared in *The New Yorker*, *The Paris Review*, *Yale Review*, *The Times Book Review* and other journals and anthologies. Seshadri has received grants from the New York Foundation for the Arts and the National Endowment for the Arts and has been awarded *The Paris Review*'s Bernard F. Conners Long Poem Prize and the MacDowell Colony's Fellowship for Distinguished Poetic Achievement. He currently teaches poetry and non-fiction writing at Sarah Lawrence College and lives in Brooklyn with his wife and son.

Praise for *Wild Kingdom*

'Vijay Seshadri's poems are wittily alive to everything, continually quick and surprising, expertly turned.'

– Richard Wilbur

'Vijay Seshadri tracks "the signature stinks and blood trails" of our species – its squalor and splendor, seen here with both charity and rage – exhilaratingly in this book. The poems have both electric energy and gravitas. Short and long poems (which is rare) equally have authority. The distinction with which this new voice deciphers the "Rosetta stone" of our "defective mythologies" is unmistakable, and absorbing.'

– Frank Bidart

'These are poems full of musical light and dark wit. Their cadences are wonderfully poised between regret and discovery. Vijay Seshadri is a lyric poet who can mix elegy and affirmation within a few stanzas of one another. He makes the landscape and the cityscape into one challenging and heartbreaking place where the old transformations of language can still happen.'

– Eavan Boland

Praise for *The Long Meadow*

'This is a strong, almost reckless voice turning dark experience into an unrelenting sense of possibility. From the rhyming stanzas to a long prose meditation, the power of casual declamation holds sway.'

– *The Los Angeles Times Book Review*

'What makes it so appealing is its formal and thematic modesty… His ability to see where the fantastic and the realistic mingle, "where matter becomes number and number matter," and to draw casually convincing distinctions gives this book its understated but gently persuasive power.'

– *The New York Times Book Review*

'Seshadri's second collection is gracefully contemporary... and effortlessly ranges from Russian Church history to Rocky and Bullwinkle.'

– *The New Yorker*

'Thematically, Seshadri asks big questions and addresses big issues – time and consciousness, suffering and devotion – but for all their deep seriousness of purpose, his poems refuse to take themselves too seriously…'

– Campbell McGrath, Head Juror for the James Laughlin Award

For my sister, Veena

Contents

THE LONG MEADOW

Acknowledgements

Grateful acknowledgement is made to the following publications in which some of the poems in this book have previously appeared: *AGNI:* 'The Refugee', 'Beginner', 'The Testimonies of Ramon Fernandez'; *Antaeus:* 'Made in the Tropics'; *Boulevard:* 'Prothalamion'; *The Nation:* 'A Sketch from the Campaign in the North'; *The New Yorker :* 'Elegy', 'Divination in the Park', 'The Reappeared', 'Locus Solus', 'Alien Nation', 'The Scholar', 'The Disappearances', 'The Long Meadow', 'North of Manhattan', 'Baby Baby'; *The Paris Review:* 'Lifeline' (recipient of 1995 Bernard F. Conners Long Poem Prize), 'Visiting Russia', 'Interview', 'Ailanthus'. *Shenandoah*: 'Too Deep to Clear Them Away', 'This Fast-Paced, Brutal Thriller', 'My Esmeralda'; *The Southwest Review* : 'The Lump'; *The Threepenny Review*: 'from An Oral History of Migration', 'A Werewolf in Brooklyn', 'Street Scene'; *Western Humanities Review*: 'Party Girl', 'My Esmeralda', 'This Fast-Paced, Brutal Thriller'; *Bomb*: 'Wolf Soup'; *Lumina*: 'North'; *Poetry Daily* (on-line):'Immediate City'; *Triquarterly*: 'Anima', 'Thelma'; *Western Humanities Review*:'Witch Elegy'; *The Yale Review*:'Immediate City'. Acknowledgment is also made to the editors of the following anthologies—*Under 35: The New Generation of*

American Poets, ed. Nicholas Christopher: Anchor Books, 1989; *The Nuyorasian Anthology,* ed. Bino A. Realuyo: Asian American Writers' Workshop, 1999; *American Diaspora: Poetry of Displacement,* eds. Virgil Suarez and Ryan G. Van Cleave: University of Iowa Press, 2001; *The Best American Poetry 2003,* series ed. David Lehman, guest ed. Yusef Komunyakaa: Scribner, 2003; *Like Thunder: Poets Respond to Violence in America,* eds. Virgil Suarez and Ryan G. Van Cleave: University of Iowa Press, 2002; *Poems of New York,* eds. Elizabeth Schmidt and Kevin Young: Knopf, 2002; *Staying Alive: Real Poems for Unreal Times,* ed. Neil Astley: Miramax, 2003—in which some of these poems have previously appeared. The author would also like to thank the National Endowment for the Arts, the MacDowell Colony, the New York Foundation for the Arts and Alice Quinn for their support.

Wild Kingdom

1

Made in the Tropics

Bobby Culture ('Full of Roots and Culture')
and Ranking Joe ('Man Make You Widdle
Pon Your Toe') shift down
in the gloaming, snap off
their helmets, kill their engines, park
one thousand cubic centimeters
of steeled precision Japanese art.
Their bands drive up
in fur-trimmed vans, unload and unwrap
the hundred-watt speakers, thousand-watt amps,
mikes and mike stands,
guitars, cymbals, steel cans,
at the Blue Room Lawn on Gun Hill Road
by the Bronx botanical gardens.
The sun over Jersey
kicks and drops
into the next of its ready-made slots,
and, like a dark lotion
from a pitcher poured, night fills
the concrete hollows, and the grass
cools in the projects,
the glowing lakes contract

around their artificial islands,
the gardens breathe
easier in the dwindling fever
of today's unbearable summer.
They say the tropics
are moving north,
the skullcap of ice melting
from both the pole now pointed
toward the sun
and the one pointing away.
But what they say is hardly heard here,
where the cooling brickwork
engine red Edwardian
railroad flats empty
their tenants, who gather
in twos and threes, float down
from the stations,
and congregate at the Blue Room Lawn
to celebrate Independence
Day in Jamaica.
The bass line fires up.
From Savanna-La-Mar to Gun Hill Road
the backwash of reggae spirals
to its perch, ripples
and flares its solar wings
along the upended moving limbs,

as if a chain were passed through every wrist,
as if a chain were tied from hip to hip.
The sun does what it does because the earth tilts.

Street Scene

The job of redemption, with its angels and lawyers,
runs late into the morning;
the halls are empty, and from sea green foyers
where aquamarine jackets sag unused
no one walks out to be disabused
by the day, so confident and businesslike.
The domiciled, stunned, paralyzed, in mourning

for the vanishing illuminations, radium-edged,
that made their nerve ends glow
in the dark, are secretly pledged
to attenuate themselves in this,
the spirit's nocturnal crisis,
and still twitch with dreamwork,
and won't open their eyes. But although

not enough energy otherwise subsists
for the nurse to pop an antihistamine
and rise from her viral mists,
for the existential tough guy and thief
to wake up to some extra grief,
for the dog to be led to the park,
for the viejo to paint his fire escape green,

so that their race might never be caused to perish
from the contradictions of flight,
up above the satellite dish
pigeons of every color but exactly one size
mob, scatter, and reorganize
to practice crash landings on the street
that divides the black neighborhood from the white.

And at a distance rinsed of charity and malice,
their riots are being umpired by
the unmentionable, porticoed phallus
of the Williamsburgh Savings Bank clock tower,
which manufactures the next hour,
serene in an ongoing function
it can never be called on to abjure or justify.

Divination in the Park

1

Under the bursting dogwoods, et cetera,
having just finished a pear for lunch,
I lie over the earth, to feel it swim
inside my posture, and sleep,

while full-bellied women pole home with small children,
and black waves fling
grappling hooks and grab by inches
the torn-off, uplifted rocks

stranded offshore like apple trees in the fog.

2

The upper parts of the earth are slowly thawing.
Less than slowly, the groundwater
rises in the crevices and exposed places,
five strata down where the fossils are.

The winter was mild. In the bulbs and empty hives
spring rubs the velvet from its new brace of horn,
and around the drowning rocks
the feral light of equinox

sheds a pattern on the ocean.

3

To think that before today, of all the days,
I was less than a snake sunning on a rock,
but that now I'm
the lord of the serpents in the temple,

worshipped and adorned in my eloquent lengths.
So what if I fail the test of time?
I cling to the earth as it banks and glides.
Miners enter my abandoned skin

with strings of lights and diagrams.
Gods on couches ring the horizon.

'Too Deep to Clear Them Away'

A woman is calling my phone for Paul.
No Paul here, lady.
No Paul, no John, no Arturo, just me
and fir and alder stumps
that stretch out like a half-buried battalion
from the ridge spine furrowed
by the wheel tracks of the yarder. Men
come here to cut and haul,
but what they cut grows on.

She calls again. No Paul, lady. Pablo!
He must have gone back to the island. Give
him up. A man lives here awhile and then
another man comes and takes his number.
And across the gutted valley under
next year's stand of sacrificial timber
the split-tongued fir cones plan
vengeance from their beds of moss.

No, I don't want to go to a movie.
I want to sit on my stump and read,
and plot, and imagine things. How,

for example, as night comes on and, grown
tired of the tunes from the buildings,
one lone window washer hangs his harness on the moon.

The Reappeared

Long after we stopped remembering, word of him
drifts back from the coast
to let us know he's still hanging on

in someone else's place and time,
living in a shed in their ivy-choked gardens—
his head shaved, his altered face,

the skin in patches under his eyes.
Supposedly, though, he's still tender and wise;
and having found out it's the same there as here—

the heat breaking out of its sack,
the stars wobbling on their black thrones—
he's made up his mind never to come back.

It's all the same; and on its verge
the borderless ocean scrawls and scrawls
reiterations which repeat

that it's all the same,
and he can fall into it and never change—
resurface, and simply swim away.

Elegy

The ambulance is gone. The squall's
ragged edge fingers
the fresh green stitchings on the alder trees.
Its belly cracks open and pours

through the timbered swale in back of the house
where, with the lights lit early,
the dangerous hours

of a slowly imploding
spring evening circle
the person left behind to answer the calls.

Friend, you're in the hands of professionals now—
shaved and scoured,
black life mask strapped to your mouth,

ampules of glycerin, plasma
by the quart, blossoming in the branches
of your temporary yard, your eyes
reflecting the oscillating lines—

and your heart's plush chambers fibrillate,
in distention darken and swell
three times their size,

swelling in one perpendicular
effort until they
collapse at last.
Friend, it grieves me that you're breaking

your promise to take me hunting.
This fall, you said, on opening day,
when the alders

are nervous with change,
you'd come to my door and we'd drive
the Upper Bay Road to the blind.

THE REFUGEE

He feels himself at his mind's borders moving
down the fifteen rows of laid-out soil
and out to the fence where the mulch heaps spoil
beside the rust-scabbed, dismantled swing
and the visions that disturb him sometimes spring
up from a harmless garden-hose coil:
the jackbooted armies dripping spoors of oil
that slick the leaf and crap the wing....

He sees each rifle as we who see him,
in the crystal blizzard of a century's static,
try to reach him with our two-bit magic.
But he escapes us to roam in the garden:
too clear to look through or distant to ask;
pinned like a flower on the genocidal past.

A Sketch from the Campaign in the North

Just before dawn the women are washing
skirts and blouses, slacks from Hong Kong,
scrubbing their cotton on pockmarked boulders,
cleaning their limbs with mud and lemons
along the turbid river.
At the edge of the jungle, in surplus tents,
the men are talking without weakness or strength
of the recent change in the government.
On the other bank the soldiers are waiting
for the sun to rise from the hills behind them,
not smoking, not talking, in place and unmoving
as the leaves above them waver.
The day unfolds as if kept in a folder
on a desk in the capital.
The sun rises and blinds the river
the soldiers line up and fire from its cover
the air is gravid with sulfur
the river takes blood without changing color
a siren signals the end of the hour
and later in the capital
word is leaked to the foreign papers—
not even their souls climbed free to safety.
There are no handholds up that wall of light.

Of and Relating To

Last week every single night was absent,
leaving an impenetrable blank,
with its smoke from burning tires
and the weak, pestilential grinding of trucks;

but tonight has gone by with a will of its own-
exfoliating, extreme
in its intricacy—
like a drowned field seen from the window

of a commuter express,
brimming with the silver of yesterday's flood,
grazed by the languid,
trailing leg

of the heron, thick with cutthroats
and newly sprung minnows
who act as if they know
how they got there.

They watch the truants, knee-deep
in the muck, and studiously avoid

the well-aimed rocks and the hooks
baited with dough balls,

and scrutinize the witch carried down in a litter
to hand out oranges and kiss off
the herons. She lets
the minnows go unnoticed.

The moon sets, flushed and fully repentant,
its two halves finally joined;
and a night that didn't
fall short of what it professed

is finally reinterred, bequeathing
several unrecognizable objects—
three peaches and a spirit lamp
scattered on the window's sunlit ledge.

The Testimonies of Ramon Fernandez

I don't want to back in and pretend it's wrong anymore—
I know it's right
to put the pedal to my appetite
until I hear the engine roar.
Alone inside my six hundred muscles,
almost personless
in an accelerating cubbyhole,
I can scale the metalled roadways
a co-conspirator of those
for whom the green lights synchronize
and are, in fact, made.
Has anyone ever said about them
they spin their wheels,
grind the vicious circle,
or go out of their way to entertain
ideas once fresh now slippery with blood?
Of course not.
And just looking at me
you can see I should be running with them.
I really should.
But that day I found a devil more subtle,
who offered me from his split mountain

not the kingdoms of earth,
with mule trains, janissaries,
merchant princes,
but fifteen acres on the Alsea River
where the road to Corvallis turns
up to the ridges
only part ruined
by the yarder and the backhoe,
and the woods hoard twilight
long after the sun
bends its attentions to Oriental nations,
leaving a mind long unreconciled dazzled
in that pure half-darkness
as it hears
the simple running of those supple waters.
Believe me when I tell you
what I stand accused of now
I would have done for much less
than that. But there was more:
Terry and Jane stood by the cistern.
The years since I'd seen them—
listless, oneiric,
walking invisible through the burning city—
the conspiracy of error, event,
and defective mythologies
that had cut me out

to be sent to the block
the way a good dingo cuts a lamb from the flock,
fell away and dissolved.
Substance stopped being visible,
or even visual,
and then I imagined that the sun
had come back, reflected
in the enormous mirror
through which the handiwork of its aeons
had continuously passed,
but so close I could abide
its gaze, and even see myself
on or about its giant acreage
of plasma no human
can seriously admonish, under
the perfection yellow
plasmic hurricanes
that deteriorate inwardly
in a process whereby
the subatomic realm is fused
with that which contains elephants,
elected officials, smart bombs,
periwinkles, cherry esplanades,
and the law of the excluded middle.
Did I give in, you ask? Did I submit
to the purity of that vision?

Is the Pope Catholic?
Tired a little of gawking
at my sudden wealth,
I turned back down to the river.
A 58-faceted diamond, blasted
from Transvaal kimberlite,
smuggled out in a miner's
large intestine, cut and polished
in an Amsterdam cellar, and stolen
from a window display
on 47th Street,
could show us no more of what we actually crave
when it comes to fire
than the water rising at my feet
and shimmering backwards
to the hundreds of tributaries,
shaping and molding this piece of the Coast Range,
which could easily have been,
according to our atmospheric sciences,
the water of the Amazon
itself, draining more of it
in a single day
that a city of twelve million
drinks in a decade.
Terry and Jane were long gone by now,

but far upstream
on a crimson bed of spawning gravel a hen salmon
dug herself in and nested
as a buck circled in the current above her.
The moon was in phase.
The mouth of the river was crowded
with urchins, kelp forests,
and rockbound stars.
The river began to levitate.
When I finally made up my mind to go
it was floating three feet above
its prelapsarian ditch.
You can shoot me if I'm lying.
Exquisite pain,
permanent sequestration in a black box
four-by-four-by- eight,
and even the 'maximum
punishment the law allows'
would be too good for me if one word
of what I've said isn't true
and doesn't constitute the force behind
the actions for which I stand here now.
I can see by your faces that
your hearts are good, and like to think
mine is, too. Believe me then,

acquit me, stand back, and let me work
there, at the water's edge,
which, as it turns out, is also
the edge of sleep.

My Esmeralda

for S.O.K.

Some people like each other and are therefore like each other,
but I like you and therefore I'm
so original a burden on my time
that all the lifeguards ring their bells
when I rise from my exclusive underneath
to wash in your England of seaside hotels,

climb my perch and send off, over the panorama
of what's most yours—those glowing herds
of prehistoric bison, sunk in clear light
up to the eyes, browsing elsewhere
extinct sky-high ferns—
my messenger birds,
speckled and superfine,
to soar the asymptotic line
that touches you at infinity. Big Mama!

Not once in any of the meretricious annals
I'm forced to read have I read
of you, nor through the maps

I have to make sense of
have I ever watched you pass.
Among words, you're the meaning of 'glass,'
and you as a river will cut your own channels.

2

ALIEN NATION

I think I'm around the wrong people today.
Though I know their cousins (who say I'm nice),
veiling their faces they tiptoe away—
some impassive, some afraid,
and others grumbling that they'd
sooner fillet me than talk to me twice.

And look! In the wind that blows where it lists,
their gun ports blazing wide open,
sail phrenic experts and therapists,
miracle workers, psyche massagers,
waving their hand-sewn Jolly Rogers.
All merciful, unthinking (but compassionate) One,

what on earth, exactly, provoked You to melt
the blanket of snow that pacified
the scrofulations of this blistering veldt
with a cold as keen and sweet
to the tongue as the coconut's meat
and made it strange enough to walk inside?

This Fast-Paced, Brutal Thriller

There's always a killer with a name like Tony,
a tie-dyed shirt, and a certain
sad history of deprivation:
just so much evil to get the plot going

down the edge of a formula
nickel-and-dimed
by years of repetition.
There's always an ocean near Hawaii or California

where the detective ponders the copy of a psalm
he once gave in commemoration
to his friend, the victim
(they shared a tin hut in Vietnam),

over whose body the salt water swarms.
Something as strange and uncanny
as Taiwanese packing twine
has been wrapped around the legs and blue arms,

giving the detective, for his deduction, a sign
that the script changed tongues

in the middle of a scene,
and only he's left to render this line

to the bored, puzzled girl on whom the camera can't focus
because she stepped over for a look
from another channel.
She stares right past him as she says, 'Jesus,

this show, it's the pits.'
And the faces start blending
on the molten screen:
screen before which the defeated imagination sits.

Locus Solus

Though they work hard to illuminate the path for us
that leads to what's such fun to call
our lonely task—ingesting, evacuating, or
coming around furious
to the justice of it all—

the unshriven but discreet, almost transcendental
intercessors of deep space—red
giants, white dwarfs, globular
clusters hanging in the cosmic vineyard—
find their rays deflected by

the arsonist panting on the rug,
the junior partner planting a bug,
the beautifully upholstered mug-

ger rekindling in front of a mirror,
the vigilante flying off to Venice
for two quick sets of tennis
at the Pro-Am Celebrity Tournament there.

Strange luck, and even worse timing:
being here and tossed on the beach,
bareheaded, barefooted, shanghaied
into feeling the climbing

elastic discomfort brought on by a universe
that we now know recoils from us, retreats
and leaves us to lurk
and grope our spongy floors,
who might as well imagine ourselves
wading the shoals at some astral Dunkirk,

so irremediably has a failure of policy and honor
stranded us between (a)
the scorched wheatfields behind us,
and (b) the burning straits ahead. No wonder
nothing shines on me as I push my cat away,

scatter my clippings, and go get my mail—
the selfsame, unsolicited communication
that arrives each morning without fail
and always reads:

'Such as were caught by the undertow
perished smilingly. The rest, of course, you know
from the particulars of our previous letter.'

A Werewolf in Brooklyn

Still almost blind in his thinking eye,
the last of the moon, as it zeros in
on the preordained spot, to modify
his downside structures and curry his skin

with its lucent brush, so the dog flares up,
he only can grasp as a metaphor.
A lozenge dissolves in a silver cup
out of which such emptinesses pour

to prove for him the Buddhists right
who say that wolfpacks of nothingness stalk
the signature stinks and blood trails of man,

but that to race with them and let them bite
will do for him much better than
Ping-Pong, kind visitors, electroshock.

The Language War

Inside the friend whose pride I injured
both one day last fall and the summer before,
the impulse thickens to even the score.
He visits my dreams, but won't say a word,

while his double bodies forth, delivered
from guilt, from doubt, and whispers together
with my victims—ex-lovers, my mother—
and pulls my hair and shouts. Hasn't he heard

yet, the jerk, that the Wall is down for good,
the Rock unrolled; that people strive to live
again, speak up, and are misunderstood;

that pen pals meet; that nations slip their fetters?
Obviously not: he won't answer my letters.
His ink is frozen, and he can't forgive.

LITTLE TREASURY OF BEST-LOVED LINES

'One might have thought of sight
but who could think of what it sees....'
Did Francis Parkman say that first,
or Bishop Pike, or Maimonides,

pulled down from his palfrey
on the flight out of Spain?
Exhausting as the effort is
to sit in the dust and unskein

these impossibly tangled legacies
of poets and whatnots, half-remembered,
strung out over an inscape
of graven images and dismembered

statues, 'where all the ladders start' –
worse than a horror show–
the hand still perforates time
to panhandle the wise, because they do know

the score, and can sing it out
with feeling. The divine afflatus,

in full spate in their brains,
justifies their priestly status

as our uncorrupted protectors
and counterweights to power, who are
gems in the respective epochs
of Timur, Dionysus, FDR,

and the Council of Twenty-three.
And the insights accrued
in their deft, precise researches—
'Hypothesize. Experiment. Conclude.'

is one well-known example, or
'We die of the cold
and not of the darkness.'—
are stamped in letters of electrum or gold

on the coins they lavish,
which the mind ceaselessly strokes
in its pitch-black hole.
'But seriously, folks,'

stop reading for a minute
and try to think about her.
She claims she hates words.
She lives alone in a condominium cluster,

shingled in cedar, its courtyards
defensible, its openings alarmed,
built just recently on land
where holsteins were once farmed.

Sometimes the alarms go off
in sequence or in chorus,
though no one's ever there.
Her dreams, too, she feels, are porous

in exactly the same way,
but since she likes guns
even less than talk, she fights
the invisible's unkillable invasions

with pyramids, intermetallic compounds,
zither music, authentic moon rocks,
and takes long particle baths
in the handmade orgone box

her ex had no room for
the day he jumped the fence.
One night she lay in a field
waiting for the harmonic convergence,

came home soaked and feverish
to throw the beef and pork
away, and clean and clean
until her house gleamed like a tuning fork.

Nothing ever came of that.
No footnotes care to mention
how her anger rusted to anguish.
But still she deserves a lifetime pension,

because, not being embittered
by the world's creepy so-and-sos,
no wave of malice has ever curled
over her, but it froze,

and never broke. So while I know
too well we should all regret
that she flutters through the meshes
of the world's iron information net,

why shouldn't we, to do her the justice
she deserves, ask ourselves if
one night she awakens,
cold and dazed, thirsty and stiff,

and sees, in shadows, an ad hoc committee
of murmurously chanting druids
calling for her sacrifice,
and swallows their concocted fluids,

could we, who write her down
for hours at a stretch,
lay our hands on her,
make her gag and retch,

though, when it comes to her body,
our knowledge compels restraint?
You tell me. 'Rescued
from death by force though pale and faint.'

Prothalamion

After telling the official in charge
of your surveillance that you won't make full
confessions, but you'll agree, nonetheless,
to sign below NO LONGER AT LARGE –
Send Pills From Now On To The Same Address,
you taxi home, amazed new owners of
something so sharply dialectical
you hardly know what else you're alive for
except to snarl, roped here, dangling above
its frantic, boiling core,
while stray dogs lick your feet, inspectors list
your damaged parts, whole families renew
their faith as they observe you spin,
and the price you pay for being you
doubles with every counterclockwise twist.
Such nameless terror, and don't I know it.
Such ancient terror, studded with foreign
instruments, freshly painted, retrofit
with missiles, lifts a robot arm to say:
Dear hearts, blessings will rain upon your heads;
your sheep will fatten, your children excel
in battle, insofar as you obey

and draw your water from this sacred well.
'What sheep?' you itch to ask. 'What well?' although,
(and I'm not trying to be mean to you)
as slick as you've been, you are indeed
fallen for good now in the well of need,
mute, mummified in love and trust;
and if you back out now you just spoil the fun
for us, your friends who have a stake in you,
and leave yourselves half-bandaged on the rack.
And think of the gifts they'd make you give back:
the rhinestone inlaid bit and spur,
the strangely boring sex videotape.
Also, you have the future to consider,
from which, the word is, you won't escape.
The public notice of your stated intent
to take each other by the hands
and drown in its flowing element
is posted there in big red letters.
Read it and weep, and then conjure with
the Rosetta stone of your creation myth.

A Preservation Society Minute

The face is gone that pushed against the window
because the window's gone:
shattered by a paving stone.
The heaviest green summer can throw

across the manmade to cover its shame
curls over the unhinged doors,
creeps along the vacant floors.
Wasps nest in the very same

chink he laid his ear on when
the strangled sounds they made
left him feeling funny and afraid.
And you want to go back? Look again?

Buy the place? Restore it? Not a chance.
For now I'd rather skip
the joys of homeownership.
And as for that pile's marmoreal romance,

I tripped on that when a ghost whirled
around on me, to half-drown me

in his ruin's slipshod eternity,
who also once came from a smaller world

only to find, after hard travel,
only the cat alive and whole,
fat on hoppers and the occasional mole,
sleeping in the circumference of a well filled with gravel.

The Gulley

I heard two shots as I slipped out across
138th Street, where the city dives
from Sugar Hill's tangled elevations
to mix it up around the lives

that wring themselves out in crack dens, temples
of learning, social clubs, and cobbled mews,
or the hushed and spotless tulip precincts
with tulips opening on their avenues

and doormen huddled under April water.
Above me, startled from high tension wires,
birds split five ways over a neighborhood
lit like a bivouac by barrel fires,

which in turn mirrored the peach-tinted lights
I tried to shield off as I craned to see
the backlit, exaggerated figure,
the nominal son of the family.

This was his night to grow bug-eyed
and jump the groove to go trash and wreck

until the morning. One punctual scream
touched a small hair on the back of my neck

before omnidirectional silence,
serviceable, unthinking, superimposed
itself on all of us who straggled there.
A window opened, and then it was closed

and latched in a third-floor flat behind me.
That was my cue to walk away.
Each needle tracking a magnetic source
could have turned one shining head my way,

to force me down the gulley's glass-smooth walls,
though for now I was free, freed by the slim
off-chance that had smuggled me between
the man who fired and whatever made him.

Party Girl

She laughs, she cries, she turns, blinking, to squeeze
his hand on his knee, which then moves to hers.
From its wild intervals, the music confers
a length of feeling, like a robe of honor
custom-made to magnify these

twain, or so it must look, as gates of bronze
they've been scratching at forever by now
open, and, in a flash, translated from
our crapulous city's sizzle and hum,
they walk like one person on empty lawns;

the shaved acres of just-cut grass, the fast-
blooming orchids, the gold light that flails
the synesthesias of a voice so green
it has to be believed to be seen,
convince them the drama is here at last,

which, soon enough, will pilot them to bed.
But can this touching of theirs really make
the itching chords resolve? Or are they
about to be cut in half? Salome,
put to the sword for the love of a head,

could tell us which if she weren't so busy
backstage. The opera over, they exit
with four eyes fixed on the direct approach,
singing, 'Bliss it was in that darkened coach ...
in the beat-up livery, off-tilt, dizzy

with the taste of supreme expectation
excruciatingly flavored by the tart
interrelationships of life and art.
But, oh, if what should happen does
a cry of love will fenestrate this nation,

and the millions, peeled of every defense,
will flood the pressess with personal ads —
'Always lonely, but sick of fads;
likes animals, sunsets; please, no smokers;
is well-travelled and has experience.'

'Let Me Play the Lion Too'

You or I could break a neck
better appointed to hang a necklace on
just from the strain of staring
inwardly at the low-tech,

age of bronze conflicts our mental parts
act out again and again.
In there, reduced in size,
a disgusted celestial being departs,

phalanxes pour fire, the trench
fills with die fallen, whose eyes
glitter and click; and 'Merde!'
I'd say if I were French

as the dust blows off to reveal
wimpled shadows stripping
the dead and our champion with
an iconoclasm in his heel.

*

Gruesome though they are, these tight
claustral spaces do draw me in

to be the mere stem of myself
in batdes I both document and fight;

but the inchwide mean streaks
I'm assigned to patrol,
from the gasping fissures of which
a mighty oracle speaks

of who we are and where we're heading,
leave you circumspect and cold.
You'd rather go out and make coalition
with the recklessness spreading

its chlorophyll through the morning glory.
Well I would too.
Let me play the lion too
and wear your skirts to tell your story

about someone burdened by an attitude
who threw his shield down and ran
from the mud and the wailing,
happily becoming unglued

in defeat, dead to this world but not yet
alive to the next, until
he stopped at a puncheon bridge
in a forest where three streams met

and stood there waiting for a few
tense minutes, to watch
a hawk in flight, and then
he crossed that bridge as I cross to you.

Beginner

When I remembered that I could see
I knew which way to look
to find the generic tree:
one ranged root steeping in a brook,

one branch the backsliding earth.
Real bark, purple finches, real gold leaf,
and, for what it was worth,
voices decent with grief

kept struggling to assert
and explain themselves.
I'd have given the shirt
off my back and emptied my shelves

of my choicest inventory
to have left that dark but growing place
before I'd heard the rest of their story
or been called to face

that life they thought would keep them sane:
rooted there like a lightning rod

eagerly anticipating rain,
scrimshawed

with warning in every human script
to remind whoever cared
that its price was pure Egypt,
and only by paying would their days be spared.

3

FROM AN ORAL HISTORY OF MIGRATION

Back in 1935 the Lord
told me, Go buy a guitar.
You be that thing, He said.
It was 6:47, almost 7:00 A.M.
The nettles and blackberry
I'd cut back the last spring
were already rooting at the stile
and bothering the chicken fence.
I was shoeing the team in the shed.
My mother called from deep in the yard:
'Run bring me a pail,' she said.
Well, you can't fetch light with a pail,
at least not our pail,
so I pretended not to hear
and kept on working.
I was good shoeing horses, I'd
rasp and trim every hoof first,
then go around and drive the half-flat nails
flat side out into shoe and hoof
with a double stroke a little like a banjo lick.
But not too deep

or you drive to the quick.
You be that thing, He said.

Some people think if you keep jumping
over a patch of ground, jump
like some bighorn sheep,
that patch of ground eventually go away.
It don't; it's always there.
Up in Harlem after the war I quit the shipyards,
got myself a Gibson and a little reputation.
I've been turning it over ever since.

THE LUMP

I was in the gaffing hatch
tying spreads of salmon gear
with a box of No. 2 hooks, a spool
of sixty-pound-test monofilament leader,

assorted plugs, spoons, and baiters—
red and copper spoons, wooden
plugs with painted eyes, E-Z
baiters I'd rig with the carcasses

of six-inch herring for the big king salmon
that graze the deepwater commons
of the seamounts and offshore reefs.
They were there to be taken,

and from Mendocino north to Canada
we'd been taking for weeks—
the one thousand antique
two-poled trolling boats

of the Oregon, Washington, California fleets
fanned out like trace hounds

on the liquid furrows
to hunt the king salmon

the Five Tribes once worshipped.
That season we were enjoying
the best harvest in a generation.
The bankers were happy,

the bartenders were happy,
and the hookers who flew in
from Reno and Portland
grinned unceasingly on every corner

of every bayfront on the humming coast.
But I was content just to
grin back, since I was involved
and, of course, we were planning

to leave the ocean for a place less scenic.
I said Rajasthan, she said Sahara,
but we knew beyond question
it was desert we were after

the minute I saved eight thousand dollars.
Eight thousand dollars
(which I imagined stacked
in eight thousand one-dollar bills)

would get us out of the wind
falling that day in sheets
from a sky rubbed albino white
and watering with static

down to a cloth-of-silver bay
palisaded by the hundred idling masts
of a bottled-up fleet
spinning slowly on its anchor chains

in frustration. Because that week
no boat was fishing.
There was a lump on the ocean
that no fisherman would try.

A ridge of high pressure coiled and uncoiled
from the Gulf of Alaska
to the Sea of Japan:
a solid wall of running weather

disappearing into space,
which the sun every morning
would peel dry of moisture
and stretch taut

and start drumming with a rhythm
the Pacific had been turning to
since time out of mind.
And down along the trench of silver

the noontime sun dug to the horizon
you could watch the lump form.
A saw-toothed running swell,
blowing off at the edges,

would break the ocean's luminous skin
in simultaneous explosions,
glittering with malice, beautiful
from a distance, and announce

a relentless northwester's arrival—
churning and blowing
until night fell,
as the days slackened to equinox,

clearing the ocean of all but the reckless,
or those clumsy giants,
tankers and freighters
that take five miles to make a turn.

*

Every year just this kind of weather
settles over the North Pacific
from July onwards,
causing, among other things,

the famous fogs of San Francisco Bay,
heat and drought inland, in
the central valleys and the mountains,
inadvertent conflagrations

on the recently logged-out units
of the fir and redwood Coast Range,
where a Forest Service worker,
dripping jellied fire from a cannister

strapped to his back to burn out
the alder brakes, salmonberry,
and miscellaneous brush from a stripped hillside,
to prepare it for planting,

can find himself, before he knows it,
stranded in a whipping brushfire.
And out on the ocean, even
in hours that are accidentally calm,

the feed scatters and the salmon lie down
and can't be fished.

Which explains why I was puzzled
when I noticed,

while storing away the spreads
of gear, the box of hooks,
the plugs, spoons, and baiters,
the crimpers and the pliers,

so I could go back home once again
and spend another evening
resting and anticipating,
hoping the weather would break,

that the boat usually moored in the slip
next to ours
was loading supplies
for what looked like a good ten-day trip.

Like our own, she was another
of the ancient
double-ended wooden trailers
built in Alaska near the turn of the century.

She was worked by a man and a woman,
with a dog to keep them company.
I'd talked to the woman once or twice—
we'd had exchanges, detached and laconic,

that anyone familiar with boats and docks
would immediately recognize.
I'd have to say that she was someone
I wouldn't have been able to fish with:

intense, attenuated, all edge
and no middle, too controlling,
as it seemed to me then,
for the warped space of a thirty-six-footer.

The dog, though, was sedate and polite.
I liked him and fed him often.
I don't remember now if
I'd ever talked to the man before that evening

but I went around then to ask him,
as casually as I could—
because I didn't want to jinx him—
if something had changed in the weather

that made them decide to try it.
He said no, not for three more days,
but that they were going anyway
to prospect on the Banks

and catch the odd fish in the mornings
before the ocean grew sloppy.

The boat was tough enough,
and they'd seen fronts like this before.

Afternoons they'd shut down
and nose into the swell.
Mornings they'd fish a little
and evenings look around,

and when the wind finally dropped
they'd be on top of the school
a day ahead of the fleet.
The lump wasn't so big to kick them over.

Because I'd heard about him that
he was circumspect and farsighted,
and also because I had no right to,
I didn't disagree; but, instead,

since I knew they'd had difficulties
during some of the best fishing –
a bent shaft, and then
a cracked prop, both requiring

expensive haulouts
while everyone else was making money–
I offered to show him where we fished,
and the gear we were using.

So I bisected a point on the charts
where we'd found a ball of feed
surging with herring and baby hake,
and told him that we followed it for days,

combing the deepwater fissures,
drilling our lines
through the boiling rips
from eighty fathoms out

to the never-seen mountains
with three port wires, three
starboard wires, two dog wires
on the bow, eight spreads

on every wire catching so many fish
we couldn't stop to clean them
and had to lay them on deck
wrapped in shrouds of wet burlap

so the sun wouldn't manhandle
the silver of their skins.
And then, when it started getting dark,
before the last pull of the wires,

we'd rip out their gills
along the gill rakers,

slit them lengthwise, gut
and scrape with a spoon the bloodlines

that wander their spines, pack
their bellies with flakes
of milk white, blue-edged ice,
lay them out in the bins

on a bed of ice, feed
the slick jewels we found inside
to pig-eyed gulls and whiskered seals,
and then pull the wires the last time.

And on that last pull,
with the coal-dark ocean poised
on the interwoven rim of twilight,
we saw, regularly,

a king salmonfish, radiating,
jump for a hook like the moon.
I wanted the same for them,
and I told them so,

and then I hopped on my bicycle
to go eat dinner over the bridge,
where I stopped for a while
to watch their boat crossing the bar

as the fog came spilling through
the broken dish of the bay
and tried to douse
the quilled lights of the harbor,

the many-colored lights of the harbor.
And I thought then, not
for the first, but, I suppose,
almost the last time,

that living outside history was best,
and that at moments like this, here,
in Oregon, I'd made it, free
and clear, standing like this

to watch a fishing boat
strobing down the line of buoys
past the No. 2 can,
the whistling can and guardian of the harbor.

*

A month passed before I found out
what eventually happened to them.
He was right; the wind
stood down three days later,

and all the boats in the fleet
ran up to Neah Bay,
grounds that from Oregon
we called the end of the world,

to fish the white-fleshed kings
that run the Frazer River.
When I came back I heard
that a dory fisherman working

the thirty-fathom line
had almost had the bow
of his dory knocked off
by their double-ender

running straight east for the beach.
He yelled from his hatch,
'You son of a bitch,'
and then looked closer

and went over to his radio
to call the Coast Guard,
who sent their forty-footer out quickly
and retrieved the boat

just before it racked up on the reefs.
The yeoman who entered

the wheelhouse, to check out
the charm bracelet, the lucky doorknob,

the pictures and postcards
from a friend in Paris,
the 8-by-12 reproduction
of a unicorn tapestry tacked

above the compass, found the dog
sleeping quietly in the fo'c'sle.
The couple had vanished.
They speculate,

because the gear was trailing
with a few drowned salmon
hanging on the spreads,
that one morning they found the school

and kept fishing as the wind came up,
and that she, while going
up to the galley, or at the scuppers
tying down a stabilizer,

was bucked into the water
by a rogue swell,
and that he jumped in after her
to try to save her

from the always funnelling currents
that take a body down
instantaneously.
Others suggest that he was the one

who went in first, losing
his footing on the rolling deck,
and that she was the one who followed
to rescue him.

But what the public explanations,
consistent as they are
with the facts we have, don't explain,
and what mystifies me still,

even though I think about them
not often but regularly,
is why neither one put
the boat in idle when he or she went after

whichever one went overboard.
The boat kept on moving
in a fast troll, made
thirty miles and almost swamped

a dory in its passion for land.
What I would have done

is throttle down the boat
and then go in

sure of a place to swim back to
win or lose.
Given that neither were amateurs,
why didn't they do that, too?

And the darker theories, the ones
that address their obvious desperation,
though they have their attractions,
seem wrong, seem unsatisfying to me.

For all we know, they might have been
transported somewhere.
And what about the dog,
an animal they loved, who,

thanks to the Coast Guard,
now lives with a family in Waldport,
a town on the Alsea River
fifteen miles from where we were.

Lifeline

As soon as he realized he was lost, that
in kicking around his new job in his head,
the new people he'd met, and how
he could manage a week in Seaside,
he'd stumbled past the muddy fork of road
that slithered down in switchbacks
to Highway 20, and now couldn't tell,
through rain clouds coarse as pig iron,
and about as cold, which languished
over each of the scarred mountaintops,
where west was, or east, or north,
or feel the sun's direction,
he stopped, as he knew he should,
and doubled back. An hour at the worst
would bring him to the International
inert in a ditch with its radiator
punctured, its axle broken, and blood
from his temple on the steering wheel.
He wished he'd never set eyes on that truck . . .
here he was, trudging like an idiot
through a thousand-square-mile dead spot
of Douglas fir, soaked to the bone

and hungry, with his head throbbing.
He wasn't up to this, he said to himself,
staring disconsolately outward
to the numberless ridges and valleys, singed
with the bitter green of the firs.
But why hadn't he reached the truck yet,
or at least somewhere familiar,
where he could get his bearings again?
He didn't recognize the ridge he was on.
He'd never seen this particular patch—
glinting with wild crocus prongs—
of clear-cut ground, torched and scarified.
Should he keep going, or return again?
There and then he made his third mistake.
Hearing, or thinking he heard,
deep in the valley below him plunged
in mist, a chain saw start and sputter,
he made off down toward the sound.
It would be a gypo logger, scrounging
deadfall cedar for shake-bolt cords,
or a civilian with a twenty-dollar permit
to cut firewood for sale at a roadside stand.
Either way, he could get directions
and hitch home by dark. Hours later,
night found him in a hollow, shouting
until he was hoarse for someone, anyone.

The weekend was almost here, and no one
at work would miss him before Monday ...
he lived alone, idiot, he lived alone
and couldn't count on a single person
to send out an alarm. Those first hours
he spent shivering under a lip of rock,
wide awake, startling at each furtive,
night-hunting animal sound, each flap
of the raptors in the branches overhead.
On the second day he lost his glasses.
It happened like this: As he struggled
over the cryptic terrain all morning—
terrain that would seem, if looked at
from high above, from a helicopter
or a plane flying low enough to pierce
the dense, lazy foliage of clouds,
created, finessed, meticulously contrived
to amaze, like a marvellous relief map
of papier-mâché, revealing its artifice only
in the improbable dramas of its contours,
its extravagant, unlikely colors—
he had what amounted to a real insight.
All this was the brainchild of water.
Stretching back beyond the Pleistocene—
how many millions of years?—
imperial rain had traced without pity,

over and over again, its counterimage
on the newborn, jagged mountains
until the length of the coast had been
disciplined to a system designed
to irrigate and to nourish the soil.
He decided he'd follow the water down.
He'd use each widening tributary
like the rung of a ladder, to climb down
from his awful predicament, and soon
work his way to the ocean—though, of course,
long before that he'd run across people.
With this in mind, he came to a stream
heavy and brown with the spring runoff,
its embankment on his side steep
to the point of perpendicularity, thick
with brush, though on the other side
a crown of ferns tumbled gently down
to the next watershed. It seemed like
a good idea to cross, and farther on
he found a logged fir with a choker cable
still attached (it must have snapped
when they tried to yard the falled tree
to the road high above) straddling
the stream. A little more than halfway over
he slipped on the treacherous wood
and would have gone in but for the cable,

which he lunged at just in time.
That was his lifeline, though flailing
to save himself, he knocked the glasses
from his head. Now they'd reach the sea
long before him, if he ever would.
He knelt down in the ferns, exhausted,
by fits growing determined never
to leave that spot. They'd find his bones
fifty years from now, clothes and ID
rotted away, a trillium poking through
his ribcage, a cucumber vine trellised
by the seven sockets in his skull.
The play of the thin, unending drizzle
on the overlapping leaves he sank below,
on the bark of the impassive trees
looming around him, grew indistinguishable
from the pulse turning loud in his head.
The bruise on his forehead throbbed.
There were rents and gashes everywhere
down the length of his rain gear, which
let the mist and the dampness in.
Beyond a scant dozen inches, the world
looked blurry, smeared bright, unattainable.
Nothing in his life, up until then
(and if this had been pointed out to him
he would have acknowledged pride in it),

suggested that anything resembling
a speculative turn of mind cannibalized
the adequate, rhythmic, progressive
movements of his thoughts and feelings.
But, still, as almost everyone does,
he'd occasionally had inklings, stirrings,
promptings, and strange intuitions
about something just beyond the radius
of his life—not divine, necessarily,
but what people meant when they referred
to such things—which gave to the least
of his actions its dream of complicity.
Now he recognized, with a shock
almost physical, that those inklings
were just the returning, reanimated echo
(on a different scale but similar
to the echo we sometimes hear in our skulls,
which leads us to the uncanny feeling
that an experience we're having is one
we've had before, at some other time—
but does anything ever repeat itself?)
of the vibrations his life made
bouncing off the things around him
sunk deep in their own being;
and that life, his life, blossoming now
in this daisy chain of accident and error,

was nothing more or less than what there was.
There was nothing hidden underneath this,
but it was small, so small, as the life
of his family was, his people, his species
among the other species—firs, owls,
plants whose names he didn't know—
all of them minute, and the earth itself,
its four billion plus years of life
just the faint, phosphorescent track
of a minute sea creature on an ocean
for the annihilating dimensions of which
words such as 'infinite' and 'eternal'
were ridiculous in their inadequacy.
He lay on his back inside the ferns
and listened to the rain's clepsydral ticking.
He tried to grasp—what was it?—
but it clattered away, that slight change
in the pressure binding thing to thing,
as when an upright sleeper shifts
just a little, imparting to his dreams
an entirely different train of meaning.
Beyond those clouds, the blue was there
which shaded to blackness, and beyond
that blackness the uncounted, terrifying
celestial entities hung suspended only
by the influence they had on one another.

And all of this was just a seed
inside a seed inside a seed. . . .
So that when, finally, late the next morning
he half-crawled out of the woods, and came
in time to a wire fence in a clearing,
less than two feet high and decorated
with gleaming ceramic insulators,
which indicated that a mild current,
five volts at the most, ran through it
to keep the foraging animals off
the newly sown vegetable garden
enclosed inside its perimeter, and saw
beyond it the sprawl of the lawn,
the 4-by-4 parked in the driveway,
the Stars and Stripes on the flagpole,
and the house, he stopped, paralyzed.
The wind was blowing northwest, the clouds
were breaking up under its steady persuasion,
but, try as he did, he couldn't will
himself to step lightly over that wire,
and cross the gardens sweet geometry,
and go up to the door and ask to be
fed and made warm and taken home.
By that small fence, he sat down and wept.

The Long Meadow

1

Immediate City

Tall and plural and parallel,
their buff, excited skins
of glass pressed to glass and steel
bronzed by the falling sun,
the city's figmentary buildings dream
that they are one with the One.
Ignoring the office workers
trapped inside their neural nets,
they orient their ecstasy
up past the circling jumbo jets.
Older than the rocks is she

across whom their shadows float.
A million rivers navigate
the necklace at her throat.
The light that falls and falls
shatters in her million prisms.
In one of her million cubicles,
a man tunes his inner mechanisms,
types an endless memorandum.
Time moves slowly, then not at all.
A boy and two girls are
trading secrets down the hall.

Visiting Russia

Another feast day, and the bells are ringing.
The bells are ringing, and not more
than a handful of versts from here,
in the garden of dead hypotheses,
Russia is rising from beds
lavish with nettles and pokeweed,
and from the stalks of fennel obscuring
the mildewed statuary.
Not more than a handful of versts from here,
closer than we thought was possible,
the Tartar ponies are pawing at their stakes,
the tents of the Golden Horde
are stretching from here to there.
Closer than we thought was possible,
Basil, Yaroslavl, the Pantokrator,
the fifth of fifty five-year plans,
the Vladimir Mother of God.
Much has happened in the years between
1200 AD and today, and it is
happening again right now.
To lighten the sleigh, a young girl
is being thrown to the wolves.

The Metropolitan is telling the Old Believers
that only with beauty can we coax
the divine into our nets.
The bones of the young girl thrown to the wolves
are half immersed in strong moonlight.
Thunder in the faraway altitudes,
vacant and subliminal,
is throwing off the rhythms
of the villagers sheaving the rye.
By the year 1200 AD,
Joseph is little more than a memory,
although threads from his coat of many colors,
along with splinters from the True Cross,
the icon, the censer, the axe, are being carried
to the taiga, the tundra, the Baltic,
flat today as a sheet of steel. A sheet of steel
incised to the horizon with faint,
steel-brushed semicircles.
A five-year plan for steel.
A region estimated to be the size
of Australia, untouched by man, rich
with fish and timber and tigers,
iron ore, bauxite, gold, uranium.
At no further cost to themselves,
Peter's cartographers have been given
the pick of the earth. The Caspian Sea,

the Aral Sea, the Sea of Okhotsk.
Few rivers traverse the steppe, its soil
is rocky and meagre, its apprehensive
inhabitants are prey
to princes, chief clerks, marauders,
Kazaks, and holy men. The feet
of their children are bleeding. Pushkin
is standing on a chair in his study.
He has just finished another stanza,
polyhedral and perfectly joined.
His thoughts stray to his faithless wife,
Natalia, née Goncharova. 'Nevertheless,'
he says to the walls, 'you're one hell of a guy,
Pushkin.' Another feast day,
and in the rye field nearest the larger dining room,
where a beautiful, archaic French
is being spoken, where
the candles have been lighted
and the table furnished with soup and bread,
a very old man is sleeping it off—
Sasha, without a tooth in his head.
When Stalin's daughter,
when Stalin's daughter
fled to Delhi, he was still there,
still dreaming of fire and sword,
rebellion and death.

INVENTORY

The pain in the clavicle. Check. The tendon
throbbing and separating. Check.
The auto-da-fé deep in the heel,

estranging the body from inside the body. Check.
The pressure rises. The lighted fuse

sizzles up the tree of nerves
and explodes in poppy blossoms,
blue blossoms of the anguished cornflower—

the body's aching pyramid
star-ypointed or dotted by
the sleepless eye. Only
the thinnest of scalpels for the transverse incision

by which will be peeled back, one after the other,
the blackening integuments, to expose
what has been waiting underneath:
'Pain (audible at noon).'

Once, in the mountains, to get away from its inflammations,
I stepped over a fieldstone fence
and walked out into a field open to the galaxy
and fell in a ditch. Ouch!

I messed up my leg something fierce.
The experience has been with me ever since.
Check. The cinder in the eye that can't be blinked out.

INTERVIEW

That was a pretty roundabout answer to what
I would have to say
was one of the more straightforward of my questions.
But to come back to this thing
you call your near-death experience.
In the accounts I've read, whose credibility,
or lack thereof,
we've already talked about—
that is, their lack thereof—
you say you saw the universe from the outside in, as,
you say, a dense web
of capillaries through which pulsed
corpuscles of light.
(A nice touch, those corpuscles.)
Guy wires, infinite in extension,
were holding down your will,
but—surprise! surprise!—you still had a will
and a body, too.
How can I breathe, without air? you asked yourself.
(I'm wondering about that, too.)
You also say . . . well, you say a lot of things, don't you . . .
You say and say and say.

When the paramedics revive you,
you say, *OK,*
so I'm not God. But neither is God.
To the literally thronging media in the hospital press room,
some of them famous themselves and so
not to be sneezed at,
with a relieved, grateful nation literally hanging
on your every word, you say,
I wish I could shimmy
like my sister Kate.
She shimmies like jelly
on a plate.
Well, I mean, really...
excuse me for living, but...
and it makes a difference, makes a world of difference...
Also, I happened to talk, while preparing
for this broadcast, to your ex, and she said,
and I quote,
Bastard. He could never get enough.
And that cameraman you slugged
outside the Royal Sheraton on your worldwide, and quite lucrative,
lecture tour? He's
a family man and a friend of mine,
and a nicer guy you couldn't hope to meet.

Witch Elegy

Over at the battlements of this misshapen edifice,
  part skyscraper and part ziggurat, I can hear them singing,
'Ding dong, the witch is dead.' They're dancing
  the dances they danced before she got here from
who knows where, and feeding a two-story bonfire
  with her inflammable detergents and salves, her furs
skinned from extinct, mythical, and unheard-of animals,
  her ivory-inlaid teak credenzas and chiffoniers.
Messengers from each of the outermost districts
  report that people everywhere are rejoicing,
and in the huts and woodcutters' hovels and
  manor houses the precious relics she hated so much
are being taken from their hiding places and caressed.
  So I guess she must really be dead, the witch,
the poor dead witch, her wings are folded now,
  and her body cognizes, as bodies are forced to,
the dark interstitial liquids of our mortal life.
  'Pity the witch,' my heart whispers, 'even though
you suffered almost more than the rest.'
  And I do pity her. Only now can I see how much
I liked her, even loved her, a little, toward the end,
  when she couldn't stave off the premonition that

she'd soon be a puddle. How often, late in my rounds,
  while barring the hundreds of windows against
the prognosticated sun, I lingered at her half-open door
  and watched while she picked her way through
the Posterior Analytics or the Almagest. She knew
  I was there. She tolerated me. Was it my imagination,
or did she learn to require my presence? Lonely, I thought,
  lonely. Though once I crept in just a little too far,
and she gave me such a look that I staggered away,
  shuddering with visions—a mound of skulls, a
necklace of skulls, skulls on pikestaffs, and other things
  too horrible to put into words, but also, recurring, intercut
with the rest, an image of sunlight on water, which
  a famous poet has written is the very picture
of Paradise. Two things about the witch no one appreciated:
  first, she was beautiful, the very opposite of her own
representation; second, she was the mistress of Time.
  She saw it the way we see the landscape, rolling
or broken, with woods or fields, until it reaches
  a town, complete with slums and palaces. Time
was the wind that blew in her hair, toward Time
  all her researches tended, and from its weeds
she pressed the elixirs that keep those of us
  closest to her as young as we are now—though
it's true that often we're inexplicably tired.

Wolf Soup

In the version of the Three Little Pigs
that I've been given to read my child,
the first two pigs, after the wolf has blown
their houses down
('Little piggy, little piggy, let me come in'),
find refuge with their perspicacious brother.
The wolf, for his part, displays no motivation,
only an impulse arrested
from his body's churning electrolytes
to demolish architectural follies.
He doesn't chase and corner the pigs.
He doesn't have a grudge against the race of pigs,
nor is he in the mood
for pig's knuckles or a nice pig's-ear taco
or even a simple ham sandwich.
And when he comes down the chimney
of the third pig's house—the one he can't
blow down, the one made of brick,
with its dormer windows
tricked out in blue, their trim
decorated with orange daisies—
he suffers for his motiveless malignancy,

in the soup pot waiting for him,
the lid of which has been removed with a
timely flourish, nothing worse than a scalding,
and runs back to his lair
somewhere over the hill.
Everyone has survived their lessons.
Everyone, as in the Last Judgment of the Zoroastrians,
is saved, even the wolf,
today exterminated
across much of the world, and almost so
in the forty-eight contiguous states.
The real story, which is locked in my desk
while I write this encryption, goes,
as you all remember, differently.
In it, the wolf eats the first two pigs,
but the third pig, the smart pig,
the shrewd, shrewd little pig, eats him in a soup
flavored with the turnips gathered
in a memorable prior episode.
Long did that pig rest a pensive trotter on the windowsill,
as he looked down the dusty road
travelled by the wolf.
His brothers were dead, his mother
unapproachable in her grief, and for weeks
the taste of wolf, at once unguent, farinaceous, brittle, and serene,
touched his mind with a golden fire.

In a pig's eye, he thought,
as his molecules began to recombine...
My son might be ready for this version of the story.
Like most four-year-olds,
he's precocious and realistic and bloody-minded.
He already knows, for example, that Jack
was nothing better than a common thief,
and has at some point observed
that giants let their fingernails grow,
sometimes to hideous lengths.

Very Simple and Like a Song

That furrow in the hill once must have been
a notch in a sheer cliff.
The land is all changed around here,
due to the work of wind and water,
but not so much that we can't think back
to what it must have been:
on the plateau beyond what must have been the cliff,
endless animal herds mollified in the sun,
kneeling and browsing,
and the lazy embankments descending to the watercourse
strewn with a little yellow flower, now extinct,
which must have resembled the celandine.
We talk in the presumptive,
but we know we can declare this much:
they were afraid,
so they climbed down the notch to this place,
more protected by far then than now.
What were they afraid of? Not
the animals but the fact of the animals,
that the animals existed,
that they themselves existed,
that everything existed when it might as well not have—

which was their one and only revelation,
which they would come back to again and again
down the hundred and fifty thousand years
and never get more than an inch farther with it than they
were now,
when all they felt was terror.
So they climbed down here and hid.
And, then, they taught themselves to bury their dead.
They felt the pressure of the nothingness around them,
and at this place they began the digging of graves,
with their flaked hand axes.
One so took to the pressure and the feeling of it
he would teach himself to manufacture
surplus dead to feed the graves.
One female taught herself to whisper.
They would someday become
Euripides, Heloise, Saladin,
Swedenborg, Nell Gywnn, Mencius,
Gandhi and Mandela,
the Pankhursts, Captain Beefheart, Dr. Dre,
and one Terry Butler,
who shook Joe Turner's hand
in a bar in Kansas City,
and shook the hand of Rahsaan Roland Kirk.
All the while, the fear
lived right beside them,

and the sound effects accompanying it were drums drumming,
so insistent, and so convenient that they
convinced themselves that everything was fine
as long as the drums were drumming,
that only when the drums stopped would they be required to worry.

LECTURE

Moving on to the next slide,
we can see, twisted and deliberately coarsened as it is,
the exact same theme,
revisited now with an
ambition and gigantism made all the more monstrous
by the still soaring line,
instinct with delicacy and intelligence,
by the palette still fresh and strange,
the siennas and umbers
and crimsons and yellows seasoned
with the crushed carapaces of iridescent damselflies.
The silence, as in a sacristy,
with little rustlings and breathings,
is still invested in subsidiary forms and minor passages of paint.
The anatomical tenderness is apparent still in the rendering of
the sexual *disjecta membra,*
which serve at the same time
both the impulse to drama and the need for structure.
Made he them male and female.
Made he them done and then undone,
only to be resurrected
(the word is not too strong)

divorced from the bodies appended to which
they once possessed function, integrity, reality.
How we long, when we
observe these vulval forms
drawn with an insane precision,
these preputial folds, these tubes and columns and placental blocks,
for the old nudes.
Where I have placed my cursor,
note the black markings—defining almost the face we know
from the thousand self-portraits—
on this amorphous blob,
this howl of paint the color of flayed skin.
They are the last remnants of this same self, the splendid subjectivity
that gave such excitement to
his Magenta period, his Geometric period,
his Whatever-I-Say-Is-Art-Is-Art
period, his several neoclassical periods, his war
period, his Babylonian,
Egyptian, and Chinese periods,
his Long-Years-In-The-Asylum period.
How strange to see him now,
as bewildered as we are,
crouched and terrified
in a petty corner of his canvas,

as his great spaces collapse inward.
Before we turn away in shock and horror, though,
we shouldn't fail to acknowledge again
that at one time
when he would pick up a stick to draw
the birds stopped their singing and waited in anticipation,
when he drew an arabesque
in the sand, the earth itself
shivered with delight.

North of Manhattan

You can take the Dyre Avenue bus to where the subway terminates
just inside the Bronx
and be downtown before you realize
how quickly your body has escaped your mind,
stretching down the tracks on a beam
until the band snaps and the body slips free and is gone,
out the crashing doors, through the stiles,
and up the long chutes,
to burn both ways at once down the avenues,
ecstatic in its finitude,
with all the other bodies,
the bundles of molecules
fusing and dispersing on the sidewalks.
Ten to the hundredth power,
bundles of molecules are looking at paintings,
bundles of molecules are eating corn muffins,
crabcakes, shad roe, spring lamb, rice pudding.
Bundles of molecules are talking to each other,
sotto voce or in a commanding voice—
'I agree with you one hundred percent, Dog';
'I looked for you today, but you'd already gone';

'I've left the Amended Restated Sublease Agreement on your desk';
'I'm going home now,
and you think about what you did.'
The ear grows accustomed to wider and wider intervals.
The eye senses shapes in the periphery
toward which it dares not turn to look.
One bundle is selling another a playback machine,
a six-square-inch wax-paper reticule
of powdered white rhinoceros horn,
an off-season-discounted ticket to Machu Picchu,
a gas-powered generator
for when the lights go out,
a dime bag of Mexican brown.
It is four o'clock in the afternoon.
The sunlight is stealing inch by inch
down the newly repointed redbrick wall.
She comes into the kitchen wrapped in the quilt
and watches as he fries eggs.
'After what just happened, you want to eat?' she says in disgust.
Will she or will she not, back in the bedroom,
lift the gun from the holster
and put it in her purse? The mind, meanwhile,
is still somewhere around Tremont Avenue,
panting down the tracks, straining
from the past to the vanishing present.

It will never catch up
and touch the moment. It will always be
in this tunnel of its forever,
where aquamarine crusted bulbs feed on a darkness
that looks all around without seeing,
and fungus, earlike, starved for light, sprouts
from walls where drops of rusted water
condense and drip.

Don't say I didn't warn you about this.
Don't say my concern for your welfare
never extended to my sharing the terrible and addictive secrets
that only death can undo.
Because I'm telling you now
that you can also take the same bus north,
crossing over against the traffic spilling out of the mall
and waiting twenty minutes in the kiosk with the Drambuie ad.
There. Isn't that better?
More passengers are getting off than on.
The girl with the skates going home from practice
will soon get off, as will
the old woman whose license to drive has been taken from her.
They will enter houses with little gazebos tucked in their gardens.
And then, for just a while, the mind will disembark from the body,
relaxed on its contoured plastic seat,

and go out to make fresh tracks in the snow
and stand and breathe under the imaginary trees—
the horsehair pine, the ambergris tree,
the tree that the bulbul loves,
the nebula tree …

2

NORTH

As if in a well a thousand dead cities deep,
all over the hemisphere
the people sleep—
their mysteries still unsolved,

their doors shut tight.
Inside, a voice croons
Be mine tonight
to their deaf selves,

deafer than the stars.
A cold front floods
down the isobars
and inches up the pipes,

silent but in motion,
inching as steadily
as an ocean
to float them through the silence,

the cold, appetizing silence,
and wash them up on a shore
of ice far to the north,
farther north than Labrador.

Fractured Fairytale

'You're coming up daisies, moose and squirrel,'
that same red-eyed, locked-and-loaded figure
intones in ten-second intervals—
blood grinning in his beard,
his finger squeezing the trigger...

But, gosh, Bullwinkle, isn't that guy the eternal recurrence of the same
reductive nemesis in whose name
the generalized life pulverizes
our beautiful particularities,
the horn of the moose and the tooth of the squirrel.
What's it all about, anyway?

'I don't know, Rock.
I don't even know that I don't know.
But if I had my druthers,
I'd just curl up by the fire with my books
—my books! —
'cause they burn so nice and slow.'

Superman Agonistes

'When my X-ray eyes look through the humans
to the need inside,
glowing red and green,
my blood cells collide,

my lungs collapse,
my cortex rebels,
and my heart wraps
a bomb around itself

and threatens to kill us both.
But I can't stay away.
I have to fly down
to watch them pray,

to watch them couple,
to watch them fight,
exposing myself
to their kryptonite.'

APHASIA

His signs flick off.
His names of birds
and his beautiful words—
eleemosynary, fir, cinerarium, reckless—
skip like pearls from a snapped necklace
scattering over linoleum.

His thinking won't
venture out of his mouth.
His grammar heads south.
Pathetic his subjunctives; just as pathetic
his mangling the emphatic enclitic
he once was the master of.

Still, all in all, he has
his inner weather of pure meaning,
though the wind is keening
through his Alps and his clouds hang low
and the forecast is 'Rain mixed with snow,
heavy at times.'

The Scholar

Illusions she didn't know she had were shattered when
she saw in the text she was cleaning up—
the corrupt recension of the now lost text—
not the cypress of heaven
or the morphology of a recurring type
or the riverbank where a god dances
but her own self's circumstances,

and not in the lover but the miserable sinner
who, as the poem trembled
to the death of its god,
drew back in fear
and so came to be noticed
by the demon who so resembled
her sworn enemy in her department,
with his bleak chin and his knowing look.
Though prodded by him she did write the book

that captured it all—god, demon, lover, avatar,
the ascension by night, the great battle,
the sobbing behind the ruined lattice—

and suspended it between her mother tongues
in the cat's cradle of her scholarly apparatus—
made from shards, really, but mysteriously there.

Anima

Not Garbo, for instance, or my wife but white, though flecks
and patches of melanin coruscate
the olive acres rising between
her breasts and her thighs,
and African ovals frame her eyes.
Twenty-eight and chemically complex,

she studies all night for her GED.
At dawn, she goes out to do
what her doctor tells her to do:
dig in her garden, where she grows
the rose they call the cabbage rose
and the huge iris they call the fleur-de-lis.

But every so often her mind goes slack
and desperate. Spectral and pale,
she walks her hills in a long black veil
mourning me—her quizzical, her other,
her bitter, prodigal, absconded half.
Where, just where, am I that I can never come back?

THELMA

We have a small place on an ugly street,
though we keep it spick and span.
I take the garbage out, but you,
Thelma, you the man—

brilliant as the velvet eye
setting off a peacock's feather,
rayed as the sun is rayed
through storming, broken weather

and gilt-edged clouds. And me?
I strip to my birthday suit
and scream out the window at the Yemeni kids,
who scream back, *'Sharmout!'*

rolling by on their Rollerblades.
You and me, Thelma, and the little squirt,
with me on the stoop
in my cap turned backward and my undershirt.

TREE

for Richard Wilbur

Three streets south of where I sit
is a city park with a plane tree in it.

From any place you choose to enter,
the tree forms the park's pole and perfect center.

Its slight, heliotropic, side-
wise bias, its height, and its wide,

rustling canopy all testify that it has won
its long negotiations with the sun,

and now simply distributes the breeze,
and keeps guard over these

ruminant people who stand before
the local memorial to the war

or sit on the benches ordering the mess
and stilling the noise of consciousness,

while the tree arches above them, serene,
mottled, magnificent, Platonic, and green.

Ailanthus

In their distorting internal mirrors,
the battered and in pain
become the dragons mauling them.
Their spirits drain

to their spleens, which manufacture
a substance, viscous, green,
that catalyzes their hearts'
colorless acetylene,

igniting their dragon breath.
Then they breathe and burn.
The ones who did them dirt
are done to a turn.

The ones who stopped to watch
are torched to black pathetic stems
by holographic Greek fire
and ICBMs.

And what happens to
those servants of the state
whose fault it all is is too
painful to relate.

Brothers and sisters to dragons! —
but only in their dreams
the mountain spews,
the fissure steams.

Elsewhere, the tree-of-heaven grows —
in deserted parking lots,
auto graveyards, abandoned
garden plots.

The wind in its leaves
is dry, arrhythmic, and sad.
Everyone, it whispers, has their reasons,
a few of which are bad.

Survivor

We hold it against you that you survived.
People better than you are dead,
but you still punch the clock.
Your body has wizened but has not bled

its substance out on the killing floor
or flatlined in intensive care
or vanished after school
or stepped off the ledge in despair.

Of all those you started with,
only you are still around;
only you have not been listed with
the defeated and the drowned.

So how could you ever win our respect?—
you, who had the sense to duck,
you, with your strength almost intact
and all your good luck.

The Day of the Sun

Arriving early at the limit of understanding,
I managed to find a good seat,
and settled in with the others,
who were fanning away the heat

with their programs full of blank pages.
The orchestra was in place,
and soon the show started.
First, deep space

rose high and flooded the stage,
immersing all the spots
where our thoughts could have fixed
if our minds had thoughts.

Which they didn't. Then
the sun came out and stood.
That was all that happened,
and ever would.

3

The Nature of the Chemical Bond

1

On our drives into the northern and central reaches of the Confederacy, my father—a scrupulous person, slow, deliberate, rule-bound, reflective, melancholy, orderly (and all of this from birth)—would suddenly become adventurous. If there was a way to get to where we were going that was innovative or idiosyncratic or held out the promise of drama, or just gave him a chance to improvise and navigate that the road suggested by common sense and the Triple-A map didn't offer, he'd be on it in a flash. When he heard—and he always heard—the words 'back roads' in his head, his inborn caution vanished. Visions of horse farms and weathered barns with Mail Pouch chewing-tobacco signs stencilled and fading on their sides and big woods with little hollows where the people lived a life that had gone on long enough to look as if it had gone on forever clouded his brain and turned him away from his dharma-ridden self. In his crisp, musical Bangalore accent, he would say 'Let us take the back roads' at some point in our trips, even though this was when the interstate-highway system was still an unelaborated sketch on the landscape, so, apart from the occasional few hours on a turnpike, most of the roads leading to our largely rural destinations could safely be called back roads. My mother eyed him with exasperation, but, in those days, when she was young and hadn't freed herself completely from inherited imperatives of wifely deference and was, besides, still daunted enough by America to keep her natural rebelliousness to herself, she usually gave in. I was in the backseat with my sister (a toddler, oblivious, often carsick), nursing a flourishing skepticism about my parents' ability to negotiate the New World. I thought we'd get lost, and we did 50 percent of the time, because the roads that looked straightforward on the map would turn out to have uncanny forks and folds and confusing crossroads. We would find ourselves on one or another of those wrong forks and have to heave the car around or drive on, sometimes for miles and miles, until we came across a gas station or a store, where my father, embarrassed but still game, would ask for directions. If the people we were petitioning to set us straight were amazed or affronted by the sudden appearance in Arcadia of a family of East Indians—something unthinkable in those years—they didn't let on. Polite and prolix, they told us carefully what to do; and once, in Virginia, on a hot August day, when I was nine, a white-haired, wet-eyed old man gave me a cold eight-ounce bottle of Coca-Cola (I can still taste it) and took me out to the back of his antique store to show me a duck pond he had built—with, he said, his 'own two hands'—which had a miniature artificial grotto and a miniature blue-washed waterwheel being turned by an artificial waterfall.

Where were we going while we were getting lost on those long drives? We were going to Civil War battlefields. We were on our way to Manassas and Antietam and Chancellorsville; to Harper's Ferry, the MacLean house, Petersburg, and the Wilderness. We were rolling through the monotonous, low-lying country between the Alleghenies and the Blue Ridge to Gettysburg, which we stopped at five times in the early and mid-sixties. We were pointing the nose of our 1960 two-tone coppertone Chevy three-speed station wagon—three-on-the-tree the transmission was nicknamed, because the gearshift was built into the steering column—in the direction of Vicksburg; though, to my father's bitter regret, we never quite made it to that sleepy river town, crucial to the canvas of the war he was painting in his head because its investiture and seizure by Grant in the summer of 1863—exactly a hundred and one years before we approached its vicinity—secured the length of the Mississippi for the Union and brought the defeat of the Confederacy almost to inevitability. We didn't get any farther than Shiloh on that trip, Shiloh of terrible memory. Whose memory, though? That is a question my father didn't, and still doesn't, ask, a question which, when lifted up and turned over in his mind, is found to be crawling on its underside with the things designed to excite his intellectual disgust—metaphysics, cultural, racial, and national identity, psychology, historicity. 'It was interesting,' he will say when I ask him what on earth he had been thinking. When pressed, he will counterattack and throw the burden of those vacant and interminable drives—with my mother mystified in the front and my sister carsick in the rear—back on me. 'We wanted you to learn American history'—though we never went to Faneuil Hall or Plymouth Rock or the Liberty Bell or Valley Forge or Colonial Williamsburg or Monticello or Fort Ticonderoga or Fallen Timbers or the Great Snake Mound, which is not far from Columbus, Ohio, where we were living through those years. And our explorations of Washington, D.C., hard by a lot of the battlefields we visited, were perfunctory, and mostly involved Ford's Theatre, Mrs. Greenhow, and the Lincoln Memorial.

It was always the War between the States for my father. Dred Scott. Stone-man's cavalry. Mosby's rangers. Bloody Kansas. The affair of the *Trent*. The *Monitor* versus the *Merrimac*. He read and re-read Carl Sandburg's biography of Lincoln and *A Stillness at Appomattox* and *Andersonville*. *The American Heritage Picture History of the Civil War*, with its beautiful reproductions of chromolithographs and Winslow Homer oils, was a fixture on his night table. He collected battlefield brochures by the dozen. He knew the odd facts: Miss Laura Keene starred in *Our American Cousin* on Lincoln's fatal night; the Empress Carlota lived on, demented in Paris, until 1927. He knew the even facts, the awful facts: six hundred and twenty thousand dead in carnage up to that time never inflicted on humankind. He rehearsed the great battlefield eloquences: *It is well that war is so terrible—we should grow too fond of it; We cannot dedicate, we cannot consecrate, we cannot hallow this ground.* By day, he was a physical chemist. By night, he was bivouacked with the Army of the Potomac. By day, he investigated the nature of the chemical bond—the three-electron bond; the partial ionic character of covalent bonds between unlike atoms; the hybridization of bond orbitals;

hyperconjugation and fractional bonding in metals; clouds of electron probabilities along that mysterious border where the atomic and the molecular realms interpenetrate, where matter becomes number and number matter, revealed to him by infrared and nuclear-magnetic-resonance spectroscopy, electron-spin-resonance spectroscopy, absorption and emission spectra. Instruments other than the human eye have articulated the properties of light: it has a dual character, wave and quanta; it has different wavelengths. Newton, Herschel, Ritter, Young, Fraunhofer, Kirchhoff, Bunsen, Angstrom, Michelson, Bohr, Benoit, Fabry, Perot, Coblentz, and Raman are some of the names by which the minds that have discovered these astonishing things are known. There exists light of wavelengths longer and shorter than the wavelengths of visible light. From discrete bands on either side of the tiny band of the electromagnetic spectrum that makes an impression on our retinas, light directed onto a sample compound of given thickness will make the atomic particles glow or will be swallowed up and leave a shadow. The glowing or the shadow (these are, of course, just metaphors) can be captured by spectroscopes (from the Latin for *appearance,* from the Greek for *to see),* in the form of spectra. These spectra my father brought home to work on at the kitchen table. In his firm, elegant script, he covered the graph paper on which they were captured in inky lines with his mathematical runes.

When he took a break, he turned to the Great Rebellion. A socialist of the mild, Fabian, Congress Party variety—Nehru and the vegetarian George Bernard Shaw were among our household gods—he might, if asked, have described the war as a socialist war, prosecuted, whatever the concomitant or efficient reasons, to eliminate capitalism's most vicious practice, chattel slavery. No one was around to ask him, though, except me, and I couldn't have framed such a question. So he was required to confess nothing. I can't remember his ever telling me anything about the Civil War that carried the faintest odor of morality or politics or interpretation. He seemed to accept unquestioningly the then (and still) prevalent notion of the war by which the imperatives of the North were balanced by the valor and passion and superior skillfulness of the underdog South, lifting the conflict beyond partisanship, beyond good and evil, clarifying it until it became a smooth, simple drama whose meaning was contained deep within itself. He fell in step with the thinking about the war that saw motives as local, and the deeper causalities subsumed by tactics, strategy, movement, battle lines, salients and bridgeheads, preponderant forces and materiel, clemencies and inclemencies of weather, and chaotic mischances and coincidences. In the books he read, in the brochures he collected, there was no interest in justification, no question of right or wrong. Everybody was forgiven in the end, except that small gallery of characters that includes Vallandigham, Quantrill, and John Wilkes Booth. This was perfect for him. It gave scope to his instinctive empiricism and his discomfort with generalities, which were suspicious with hidden and untenable assumptions. The Civil War was as fundamental, as immutable, as the submolecular realm, a modernist war made for the modernist he was then, and still is, as clear and impenetrable as a line by Wallace Stevens or a Calder mobile. It referred to nothing but itself. Wrapped in its structures, though, was a human heroism pure and appalling and desperate, so pure and appalling and desperate that it, too, seems immutable. This was something my father understood. These were the desperate frequencies that set his atomic particles vibrating. He had been orphaned of his father at an early age in a cholera epidemic that almost took him away at the same time (he'd also survived smallpox). His family had been thrown into poverty and a humiliating dependency. They hadn't experienced the most terrible Indian destitution, but India has many destitutions, and they always heard one or another coughing and shuffling outside their door. His education had been financed entirely by the scholarships and fellowships available in what was then the princely state of Mysore—which may have been the most advanced of the Indian princely states in the decades before Independence—and in the world beyond. If the massive silence that lies at the center of his psyche is any indication, his character had not only been defined but pretty much exhausted by frugality, anxiety, and constant labor. His one chance—his one grace—had been science. He once said to me, in wonder rather than bitterness, 'If I hadn't found science, I would have been nothing.'

Hundreds of thousands of men throwing themselves against the merciless fire of a technology that had left the tactics of their officers far behind. The desperation. 'Fundamental and astounding,' Lincoln called it, meaning that even he had no words. The self moves beyond dread and terror and confronts its essential poverty and nakedness and isolation. This my father understood, too well and too immediately. The conflict was vivid to his moody, wordless fatalism, his sense, so strange in the bountiful Middle America of the early sixties, that all choices narrowed to one choice, which wasn't a choice at all but was construed as such by our incorrigible gift for deceiving ourselves into thinking we're free. And so, the following, suitably edited to disguise their violence, became the bedside anecdotes of my childhood's middle years: in the twilight of early May, a mistaken fusillade from his own men cuts down Stonewall Jackson, out scouting the enemy lines (Lee, my father says, will miss him at Gettysburg); the citizens of Cherbourg come down to the quays to watch the *Alabama* and the *Kearsarge* trading broadsides in the harbor (eventually, my father says, the captain of the *Alabama* will strike his colors and then throw himself overboard); Forrest's cavalry harasses the flanks, exploding out of the woods and forcing the Union soldiers to scatter across the deadfall and the scrub; in one half hour, after a blundering delay by his generals, Grant loses seven thousand men, dead or maimed. These stories had no interest for me when I was a kid. Their ontology was all wrong. Their being was continuous with the being around me. They took place in a terrain undifferentiated from the terrain we inhabited. The fields and woods were the same fields and woods we saw and knew, except for the fact that they were in Virginia or Tennessee. We knew people in Columbus whose great-grandfathers had been Union soldiers, which excited my father but, secretly, depressed me because of its quotidian lack of access to the different geographies where conflict and war, I thought, quite reasonably, should occur, places like the ones in the movies I loved—Ardennes *(Battleground)*, medieval England *(The Adventures of Robin Hood)*, or full fathom five in the Pacific Ocean *(Run Silent, Run Deep)*. When my father walked me over battlefields, instructing me about unwavering lines and salients, I felt as heavy as mercury, inert, bored, baffled, as baffled as I was when, years before I had the requisite mathematical knowledge or skill, he sat me down and with excruciating patience explained the concept of a limit and the mysteries, stunning to me now but impossible then, of the fundamental theorem of calculus. I did, though, understand something in those excursions. I took something away. Something came along, prodigious as a revelation. I understood him, my father. I developed a precocious awareness of his difference. And I felt guilty about having seen him as he really was. I understood something about him that a son should probably not understand about a father, at least not at that age. The passage to America had, happily for him, thrown him free, but it had also stripped him down to his naked soul. Almost to this day, like the sons of Noah, I have longed to walk backward and cover up the nakedness, the drunkenness of his intellectual obsessions, his naked, unheard-of obsessions, irritably reaching after fact and reason to fold him back into motives less uncanny and more reminiscent. Occasionally in recent years, I have engaged him in the game of Twenty Questions with which he tends to deflect assaults on his privacy.

'Was it America, Dad? Was it because you liked America?'

'No. It wasn't America.'

'Was Lincoln like Gandhi? They were both assassinated, right?'

'No. Gandhi was religious.'

'Was slavery like Untouchability?'

'That was India. This is America.'

'Did it remind you of the war in the Mahabharata? That was a fratricidal war.'

'The Mahabharata is just a story.'

2

My parents didn't go on vacations when they were young in India before and after the Second World War. India hadn't yet experienced the benefits of industrialization. Time wasn't broken up into units that represented work and leisure. Rest for the body and the soul was found in the many religious festivals that dot the Indian lunar calendar, and that bear the stamp of a cyclical rural life and an ancient nature-worshipping religion: Sankranthi, in January, the rice-crop festival; Shivarathri, in February, when the males of Shaivite families fast all night in the temple, and Shiva, creator and destroyer, the embodiment in the Indian imagination of time itself, brushes against their inner life; Ugadi, in March, the new-year festival, which my mother's feast-loving family—like my father's from a Tamil-speaking community in

Bangalore, a Kannada-speaking city, where the new year falls on a different day than in Tamil Nadu—would celebrate not once but twice; Ramanavami, in June, the birthday of Rama, famous in South India for its day- and nightlong music concerts; the birthday of Krishna in August, Gokulashtami, a long fast followed by a feast at midnight on the appointed day, the moment of Krishna's birth; Ganapathi, in early October, the festival of Ganesh—fat, affectionate, elephant-headed god who eases the passage from life to death; and, finally, in late October and early November, the dates determined by the phases of the moon, the two great harvest festivals— Navarathri, when for nine nights the *grahas,* the elements that make human life possible, among them earth, water, fire, the implements of the field, and the benisons of the cow, are given a grateful devotion; and Depavali, the festival of lights, dear to my mother's heart because when she was a girl her father, who was the chief engineer for Mysore state, would every year be invited with his family to the festivities at the rococo palace of the Wodeyar Maharajah of Mysore.

The closest my father ever got to the rococo palace of the Wodeyar Maharajah of Mysore was a brother-in-law of his who for a while owned a small bakery that sometimes supplied the royals with bread. This brother-in-law, the only source of income in my father's family after the death of my grandfather, decided one day to run off to Bombay with a young girl of his acquaintance, forcing my father's sister to move back to my grandmother's crowded, anxious household. When my mother rhapsodizes about the feast of Depavali at the palace, with its army of cooks, its opulent service, its spectacular illuminations and fireworks—or when she describes the great yearly *darbar* where her father, dressed, along with the other servants of the crown, in a black silk waistcoat and a turban, offered his prince a silver rupee as a token of his fealty, and was subsequently reendowed with the same coin by that generous, farsighted sovereign—my father can be counted on for a snort of derision. He is partial, though, to South Indian vegetarian cooking, and, like all people who have been truly poor, thinks of food as the ultimate wealth. So he fell in with my mother's desire to recreate at least some of the feasts of her youth. In those years, the only store in America that sold authentic Indian groceries was Kalustyan's, on Lexington Avenue, in Manhattan. From 1961 to 1968, we drove to New York every summer to shop there, staying with a physicist friend of our family who worked at Brookhaven National Laboratory, on Long Island. With the Chevy loaded down with supplies for a year—hundred-pound burlap sacks of rice, ten-pound bags of every kind of lentil and pulse, little vials of precious Kashmiri saffron, ginger roots in the dozens, crystals of camphor, tens of thousands of black mustard seeds, chilies, fresh and dried, fresh and dried coconut, coriander, seed and plant, peppercorns, rock candy, dried curry leaves, cardamom, fenugreek, asa-fetida, Japanese eggplants, and Chinese melons—we would drive back to Ohio. On the Pennsylvania Turnpike that first time, my father saw a sign pointing to Gettysburg. He decided to turn off and take a look, and liked what he saw. This was what set him off, the Aristotelian efficient cause. On each trip to New York after that, until my mother put a stop to it, we would visit the battlefield. During one trip, we went to Gettysburg twice, on the way east and again on the way back west because he had seen in a bookstore in Manhattan a photograph of a Confederate sniper's nest built from rocks and wanted to find out if it had been preserved.

'We have been here already,' my mother said. 'We have been here ten days ago.'

3

We were strange. We were doubly strange: strange because Indians are strange even in India, having been exiled from time and history by an overdeveloped, supersaturated civilization, and strange also because no one remotely resembling us had ever before lived where we lived. But I was the only person in my family beset and burdened by this strangeness. My parents were absorbed in the details of our material and spiritual survival—my mother, gregarious and active, was busy with her intense domestic arrangements; my father was either working on his spectra or off with the Army of the Potomac. I, though, was transfixed by our image reflected in the order that surrounded us. As painful as it was to look, I couldn't in those days tear myself away; and I became trapped by what I saw us as in the mirror of our benign, distant, Protestant Midwestern world. I was like Shakespeare's liquid prisoner pent in walls of glass, and eventually had to ooze my way free through the cracks formed in that glass by the earthquakes of the 1960s. This confused us as a family, forced us to expend psychic resources we had always carefully husbanded, and made us all unhappy, especially my father, who had wanted me to climb up, climb up to his impossible level of concretion and discipline. I didn't come back to the Civil War for a long time. But then, slowly, peculiarly compelled, I did, watching the documentaries on public television and browsing in the history shelves of libraries and bookstores. I kept this resurrected interest secret from my father for years. One Thanksgiving in the mid-1990s, though, when I thought I was safe, I mentioned that I'd recently read Shelby Foote's account of Gettysburg, and was surprised at how clearly I could visualize the battle, and see it unfold hour by hour. He didn't say much at the time. His response was delayed, and when it came it was calculated and massive. Three weeks later he sent me a Christmas present, a first edition of the two volumes of the *Personal Memoirs of U. S. Grant.* When I called to thank him, I told him that Gertrude Stein had had a high appreciation of the memoirs. He said that was good, and that he might read Stein (he never did). And then, with both of us recognizing that the long interregnum had finally ended, that we were stuck with each other, we got into it about Grant. Grant was fine until he became president, I said, but what a terrible president. The corruption! The railroads! This agitated him. It wasn't Grant's fault, he couldn't be held responsible for his corrupt companions. The Civil War had brought changes that no one could have encompassed, not even Lincoln. Look at how right

Grant was about the Mexican War. Look at how he wrote those memoirs while he was dying of cancer, in order to provide for his wife. That alone was enough to wipe away the blemishes of his administration. Grant was always impressive. His only fault was that he was too trusting. Grant, my father said, had requited himself. Grant, my father insisted before we hung up, was an underestimated man.

4

THE DISAPPEARANCES

'Where was it one first heard of the truth?'

On a day like any other day,
like 'yesterday or centuries before,'
in a town with the one remembered street,
shaded by the buckeye and the sycamore—
the street long and true as a theorem,
the day like yesterday or the day before,
the street you walked down centuries before—
the story the same as the others flooding in
from the cardinal points is
turning to take a good look at you.
Every creature, intelligent or not, has disappeared—
the humans, phosphorescent,
the duplicating pets, the guppies and spaniels,
the Woolworth's turtle that cost forty-nine cents
(with the soiled price tag half peeled on its shell) —
but, from the look of things, it only just happened.
The wheels of the upside-down tricycle are spinning.
The swings are empty but swinging.
And the shadow is still there, and there
is the object that made it,

riding the proximate atmosphere,
oblong and illustrious above
the dispeopled bedroom community,
venting the memories of those it took,
their corrosive human element.
This is what you have to walk through to escape,
transparent but alive as coal dust.
This is what you have to hack through,
bamboo-tough and thickly clustered.
The myths are somewhere else, hut here are the meanings,
and you have to breathe them in
until they burn your throat
and peck at your brain with their intoxicated teeth.
This is you as seen by them, from the corner of an eye
(was that the way you were always seen?).
This is you when the President died
(the day is brilliant and cold).
This is you poking a ground-wasps' nest.
This is you at the doorway, unobserved,
while your aunts and uncles keen over the body.
This is your first river, your first planetarium, your first Popsicle
The cold and brilliant day in six-color prints—
but the people on the screen are black and white.
Your friend's mother is saying,
Hush, children! Don't you understand history is being made?
You do, and you still do. Made and made again.

This is you as seen by them, and them as seen by you,
and you as seen by you, in five dimensions,
in seven, in three again, then two,
then reduced to a dimensionless point
in a universe where the only constant is the speed of light.
This is you at the speed of light.

BABY BABY

Choices have been made that I had nothing to do with—
mistakes have been made,
and, worse than that,
Death has been served tea and fresh figs.
I was not present in that room,
at the table polished with citron oil.
I did not take part in the extended discussion
whereby the decision was refined.
So don't point a finger at me someday.
I was here by the crib, looking at you
chewing your toes,
blowing raspberries,
blowing little thought balloons
with your labials, fricatives, glottal stops, and retroflexes,
your mint-condition neurons firing.
(The language can't be understood,
but the purpose is plain.)
I was here advising you that even though
all the women want to stroke you
and all the men want to be your pal
you should probably start developing

your own resources.
Popularity like that never lasts.
I was saying how difficult it is to be
courteous, loyal, thrifty,
brave, cheerful, obedient, and wise
separately, let alone all at once.
I was pointing you far into the future, to the day
you go down to the river
and wade out knee-deep in the sacred element
and turn and see on the riverbank
seven luminous beings lined up and looking at you.
To which of them will you put your question
when you wade back? The Christians say
the story of the universe is the story of a boy and his dad.
They are absolutely right.
I can see that now, waiting here
for the smiles I'd kill for,
watching you as you sleep curling your fist,
which in a time I can barely recollect
did not, or maybe did, exist.

THE PAINTED THINGS

Never as slowly as you do now
have I seen you take the painted things off before.

One hour isn't enough for the bangle on your wrist,
one day for your jewel-encrusted breastplate.
One night dies
expecting your velvet garter.

The glacial tick in the moraine,
the clock of radium in the stone
can't keep the time it takes for your sky blue blouse
to be slipped from your shoulder.

And as for your *sous-vetements*—
the sun will burn out before
I can put my paws on those,

sleeping on my paws at your little desk
as I wait for you,
because I have eyes slow enough for you,
I have the eyes to wait for you.

A Fable

The boy and the father walked beside the donkey.
The road was gray, and dust rose to its vanishing point;
gray dust choked the leaves of the few
asthmatic cottonwoods along the dry creekbeds.
The sky was hot to the touch.
'Why not ride the donkey, as it's so hot?'
passersby on the road suggested.
The boy and the father whispered to each other.
(They were more like brothers
than they were like son and father.)
The father got up on the donkey.
Other passersby, or maybe the same ones
doubling back—the only leisure-time activity
in that part of the world involved
walking up and down the dusty road—
said, 'Selfish, selfish old man! Think of your boy,
whose legs can't bear the insult
of this road, let alone the heat's.'
They went on a ways the way they were,
because they didn't want what scrutinized them
with such detachment to think they were slaves
to public opinion. Then they traded places.

A mile later, an old woman on a porch, rocking
and shading her eyes from a sun that seemed
not to dwindle but instead hammered
the sky to a thinness irreconcilable
with the laws of nature, shouted out,
'Worthless! Letting your old father walk!'
So the father climbed up behind the boy,
and they both rode the donkey.
This incited an animal lover,
wearing a hat like the ones you see
in the wood-block prints of the Japanese,
to screaming flights of invective
for burdening the donkey with two bodies. So,
abashed, they got down, and they carried the donkey.
The donkey howled and evacuated in terror,
but they carried him anyway, over the undulating road
and across the boulder-studded arroyos.
They came to a town and lived there for a while,
and then moved to a larger town, and then
to the fabled city, suspended
on a plain between two mountain ranges.
They lived in a room in a house in a suburb
known for its featurelessness,
the two of them, with the donkey.
The father couldn't work anymore—
the business with the donkey had broken him forever—

so the son went out alone in the world.
He was the one who buried the donkey,
in the dead of night, when no one was looking.
Later, he buried his father, too,
but this time in daylight, in a decent graveyard.
He didn't care about his place in the world,
but he married a woman who did, and had children
and prospered, in a manner of speaking.
The tally of the generations begins with him
and extends down the centuries
and across the hemispheres
and numbers CPAs and bookies,
coopers and wheelwrights,
neurologists, embezzlers, claims adjusters,
and linemen for the county.
And, though diverse and ignorant
of one another, though pressed like grapes
through the bewildering human genotypes,
each of them has this one thing in common—
each knows, obscurely, unconsciously,
without knowing how he knows, that
only the complicated, ambiguous victories
are worth having, those that take place
under the sun, above
the boulder-studded arroyo,
with the dust, grayer than bone, rising on the road.

The Long Meadow

Near the end of one of the old poems, the son of righteousness,
the source of virtue and civility,
on whose back the kingdom is carried
as on the back of the tortoise the earth is carried,
passes into the next world.
The wood is dark. The wood is dark,
and on the other side of the wood the sea is shallow, warm, endless.
In and around it, there is no threat of life—
so little is the atmosphere charged with possibility that
he might as well be wading through a flooded basement.
He wades for what seems like forever,
and never stops to rest in the shade of the metal rain trees
springing out of the water at fixed intervals.
Time, though endless, is also short,
so he wades on, until he walks out of the sea and into the mountains,
where he burns on the windward slopes and freezes in the valleys.
After unendurable struggles,
he finally arrives at the celestial realm.
The god waits there for him. The god invites him to enter.
But, looking through the glowing portal,
he sees on that happy plain not those he thinks wait eagerly
for him—

his beloved, his brothers, his companions in war and exile,
all long since dead and gone—
but, sitting pretty and enjoying the gorgeous sunset,
his cousin and bitter enemy, the cause of that war, that exile,
whose arrogance and vicious indolence
plunged the world into grief.
The god informs him that, yes, those he loved have been carried down
the river of fire. Their thirst for justice
offended the cosmic powers, who are jealous of justice.
In their place in the celestial realm, called Alaukika in the ancient texts,
the breaker of faith is now glorified.
He, at least, acted in keeping with his nature.
Who has not felt a little of the despair the son of righteousness now feels,
staring wildly around him?
The god watches, not without compassion and a certain wonder.
This is the final illusion,
the one to which all the others lead.
He has to pierce through it himself, without divine assistance.
He will take a long time about it,
with only his dog to keep him company,
the mongrel dog, celebrated down the millennia,
who has waded with him,

shivered and burned with him,
and never abandoned him to his loneliness.
That dog bears a slight resemblance to my dog,
a skinny, restless, needy, overprotective mutt,
who was rescued from a crack house by Suzanne.
On weekends, and when I can shake free during the week,
I take her to the Long Meadow, in Prospect Park, where dogs
are allowed off the leash in the early morning.
She's gray-muzzled and old now, but you can't tell that by
the way she runs.